# *woven*
## LEATHER BAGS

# STACKPOLE BOOKS

Published by Stackpole Books
An imprint of The Rowman & Littlefield Publishing Group, Inc.
4501 Forbes Blvd., Ste. 200
Lanham, MD 20706
www.rowman.com

Distributed by NATIONAL BOOK NETWORK
800-462-6420

Photography: Yasuo Nagumo and Wataru Nakatsuji
Styling: Hiroe Kushio
Design: Yukie Kamauchi, Natsuko Ishigami (GRiD)
Illustrations: WADE Co. Ltd
Editor: Chie Muramatsu (CreSea)

English Translation: Eri Henderson
English Language Editor: Lindsay Fair
English Edition Designer: Arati Devasher

British Library Cataloguing in Publication Information available

Library of Congress Cataloging-in-Publication Data available

ISBN 978-0-8117-3823-1 (paperback)
ISBN 978-0-8117-6824-5 (e-book)

 The paper used in this publication meets the minimum requirements of American National Standard for Information Sciences—Permanence of Paper for Printed Library Materials, ANSI/NISO Z39.48-1992.

Printed in China

# woven
## LEATHER BAGS

## HOW TO CRAFT AND WEAVE
## PURSES, POUCHES, WALLETS
### *and More*

### NAOKO MINOWA

**STACKPOLE
BOOKS**
Guilford, Connecticut

Are you interested in creating beautiful, high-end bags and accessories, but find yourself intimidated about working with leather? Then, this is the book for you! In fact, I'll let you in on a little secret: I'm not a leather craft artist. I'm actually a textile artist who spends most of her time dyeing and weaving yarn.

A couple of years ago, I developed a finger weaving technique to teach my students how to weave without a loom. This led me to explore weaving with unconventional materials, including leather strips. Once I started weaving with leather strips, I couldn't stop!

Leather strips have a consistent width, making them easy to weave, and the finished product is a professional looking textile that won't fray like fabric or yarn. You can even add metal hardware, like snaps, clasps, and rivets, for stylish design elements.

The most amazing thing about weaving with leather strips is that you don't have to worry about sewing through leather. All of the bags, pouches, and other accessories in this book feature unique construction methods that allow you to create gorgeous leather craft projects without the need for specialized tools or an industrial sewing machine. And best of all, the projects themselves are beautiful in their simplicity.

— **Naoko Minowa**

# CONTENTS

Key Caddy & Card Case 2

Square Toggle Pouches 3

Classic Coin Purse 4

Kiss Clasp Pochette 5

Colorblock Mini Tote 6

Bow Clutch 7

Slim Clutch & Tablet Case 8

Gusseted Mini Purse 10

Textured Slouch Bag 11

Document Folio 12

Eyeglass Case 13

Envelope Clutch 14

Heart Pochette 15

Classic Cat Purse 16

Library Tote 18

Tools & Materials 20

Leather-Weaving Techniques 22

    Basic Weaving 22

    Braid Weaving 24

Finishing Techniques 34

    Adding a Lining 34

    Hand Stitching a Seam 36

    Installing Metal Hardware 38

    Making Leather Embellishments 44

Project Instructions 47

Design Your Own Projects 94

Resources 100

# KEY CADDY & CARD CASE

Upgrade your accessories and get organized with these helpful little cases. The key caddy features a metal fob to keep important keys at hand, while the card case is just the right size for membership, credit, and business cards. This set makes a lovely gift for both men and women.

Instructions on pages 48 and 50

# SQUARE TOGGLE POUCHES

These simple carryalls are made with the braid weaving technique and feature handmade toggle buttons. Just change the width of the leather strips to produce the different size variations.

Instructions on page 52

# CLASSIC COIN PURSE

This oversized coin purse is useful for storing change and other essentials. Refer to the guide on page 41 for step-by-step instructions for installing a metal purse clasp.

Instructions on page 54

# KISS CLASP POCHETTE

Featuring a gradated checkerboard pattern with shades ranging from beige to dark brown, this design really complements the basic leather-weaving technique. This sophisticated little bag is perfect for travel, special occasions, or even just running errands!

Instructions on page 56

# COLORBLOCK MINI TOTE

Add a pop of color to your wardrobe with this cute mini bag featuring a two-tone color scheme. The decorative handle design utilizes metal rivets for increased durability.

Instructions on page 58

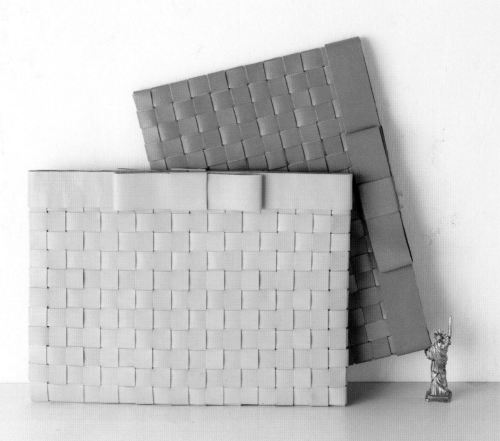

# BOW CLUTCH

This feminine clutch makes for an elegant addition to any outfit.
The design features a magnetic snap, so all of your belongings
will stay safely stored inside.

Instructions on page 60

# SLIM CLUTCH & TABLET CASE

Showcase the houndstooth and checkerboard weave patterns by selecting contrasting colors of leather strips—metallic silver and deep navy create an elegant evening look, while crisp white and lime green are perfect for a fresh daytime look.

Instructions on pages 63 and 65

# GUSSETED MINI PURSE

These cute little purses are all constructed with the same basic weaving technique, yet each possesses a unique pattern based on the starting arrangement of the leather strips. Refer to the guide on page 98 for more information on the variety of patterns that can be created by weaving with different colors of leather.

Instructions on page 67

# TEXTURED SLOUCH BAG

The slouchy shape of this bag highlights the contrast between the shiny leather front side and supple suede reverse side of the strips. The creative use of a metal purse clasp creates a dramatically arched handle and adds to the unique silhouette of this design.

Instructions on page 73

# DOCUMENT FOLIO

Woven from leather strips of varying widths, this folder is guaranteed to make your desk or briefcase more stylish. Metal corners provide structure and help keep your papers safe and neat inside.

Instructions on page 76

# EYEGLASS CASE

Use this small pouch to store eyeglasses, pens, or craft supplies.
The button and string closure allows you to customize the fit.

Instructions on page 78

# ENVELOPE CLUTCH

This elegant handbag is perfect for a night on the town. Special details, such as metallic leather, contrast binding, and tassel embellishment, provide a touch of glamour!

Instructions on page 82

# HEART POCHETTE

Fall in love with this sweet little purse! The body of the bag is constructed using the braid weaving technique, then trimmed to fit the curved clasp, revealing the adorable heart shape.

Instructions on page 84

# CLASSIC CAT PURSE

Despite its whimsical shape, this playful purse possesses an air of sophisticated elegance when woven in neutral shades like black or tan. As you work this unique, three-dimensional construction method, you'll watch this bag take shape before your very eyes!

Instructions on page 86

# LIBRARY TOTE

With its boxy shape and sturdy handles, this classic tote is perfect for carrying books. The two variations pictured here showcase the unique patterns that can be created by weaving with leather strips of varying widths.

Instructions on page 92

# TOOLS & MATERIALS

All of the projects in this book are woven by hand—you don't need any fancy looms or specialized equipment. The projects in this book are made with precut leather strips. Using precut leather saves time and creates a professional-looking finished product. Refer to the resources guide on page 100 for more information on the tools and materials used in this book.

## TOOLS

### GRAPH PAPER
Work on top of graph paper to keep your weaving aligned properly and to measure as you work. You can purchase large sheets or rolls of graph paper at office supply stores.

### CELLOPHANE TAPE
Use to temporarily hold strips of leather in place while you work.

### DOUBLE-SIDED TAPE & MASKING TAPE
Use heavy-duty double-sided tape to finish the ends of the leather strips and masking tape to prevent your work from unraveling.

### SCISSORS
Use to cut leather, lining fabric, and other textiles.

# MATERIALS

## FAUX LEATHER STRIPS

Today's imitation leather is soft and easy to handle with a texture similar to the genuine artifact. 1¼ in (30 mm) and ⅝ in (15 mm) wide faux leather strips were used for the projects in this book.

## GENUINE LEATHER STRIPS

Made from calf or lamb, authentic leather strips are available in a variety of colors and textures. ⅝ in (15 mm) wide genuine leather strips were used for the projects in this book.

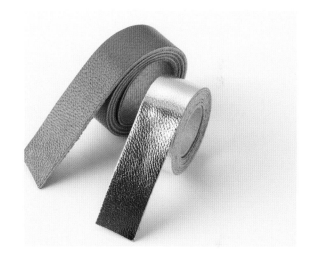

## SUEDE CORD

Thin suede cord can be used to provide colorful contrast within a woven design. You'll find a wide range of colors available in both genuine and imitation suede. Look for ¼ in (5 mm) wide suede cord for the projects in this book.

# LEATHER-WEAVING TECHNIQUES

This book uses two different weaving techniques: basic weaving and braid weaving. Each technique creates unique pattern features and requires different finishing methods. The following guide explains each weaving method in detail.

## BASIC WEAVING

With the basic weaving technique, you'll fold the outermost warp (vertical) strip and use it as the weft (horizontal) strip. This produces a diagonal checkered pattern. With this technique, the wrong side of the leather is visible in the finished work, adding contrast and texture to the weaving.

Work on top of graph paper to keep the edges of the work straight as you weave.

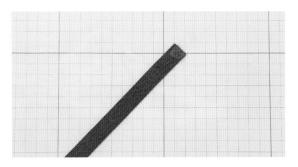

**1.** Align a leather strip at a 45° angle with the right side facing up. Use cellophane tape to temporarily secure this strip in place.

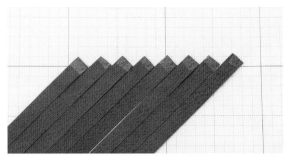

**2.** Follow the same process to arrange and secure the necessary number of strips (refer to your individual project instructions).

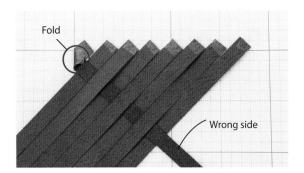

**3.** Fold the leftmost strip under. If necessary, use tape to secure the fold in place. Alternately weave this strip over and under the other strips as shown.

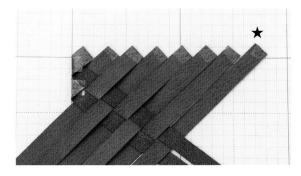

**4.** Using the new leftmost strip, follow the same process to weave the next row. Note how this strip will travel over and under the opposite strips as in step 3.

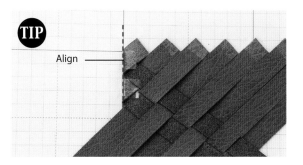

Take care to align the folds along the left edge of the work. Use the grid lines on the graph paper as a guide.

**5.** Now, go back and weave the upper right corner of the work: First, untape the top of the rightmost strip (marked with a ★ in step 4) and fold it under so the wrong side is facing up. Alternately weave this strip over and under the other strips, working toward the upper left corner.

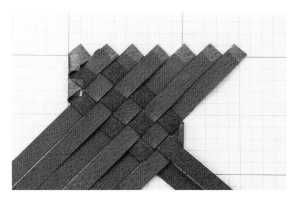

**6.** Completed view of the rightmost woven strip.

**7.** Follow the same process to finish weaving the upper right corner of the work. Take care to align the folds along the right edge of the work.

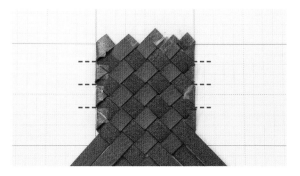

**8.** Using the leftmost strips, weave the third and fourth rows. Take care to align the folds on the left and right edges of the work. This photo shows the work after the fourth row has been woven.

**9.** Next, use the new leftmost strip to weave the next row, working toward the bottom right corner.

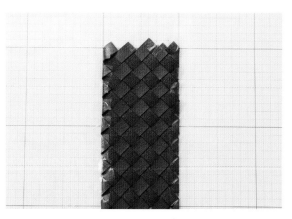

**10.** Now use the rightmost strip to weave the next row, working toward the bottom left corner.

**11.** Alternately weave the leftmost and rightmost strips until the work reaches the desired length.

# BRAID WEAVING

With this technique, the warp (vertical) and weft (horizontal) strips are separate. This produces an even checkered pattern. With the addition of a self-adhesive lining, you can use this technique to weave a three-dimensional bag without sewing. Refer to page 34 for more information on self-adhesive fabric used to create linings. Note that the braid weaving technique is worked with the wrong side of the leather strips facing up.

## METHOD #1: WEAVING A LINED BAG WITH UNFINISHED EDGES

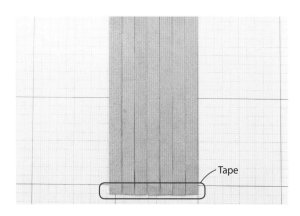

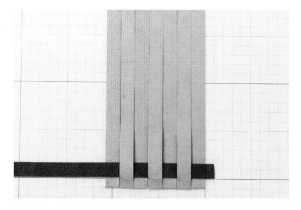

**1.** With the wrong side facing up, arrange the necessary number of warp (vertical) strips (refer to your individual project instructions). Use cellophane tape to temporarily secure the strips along the bottom.

**2.** With the wrong side facing up, alternately weave the first weft (horizontal) strip over and under the warp strips. Leave the weft strip extending about ⅜ in (1 cm) beyond the right edge and secure with tape.

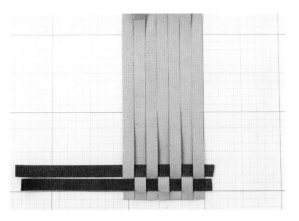

**3.** Alternately weave the next weft strip under and over the warp strips. This strip will travel under and over the opposite strips as in step 2.

**4.** Repeat steps 2 and 3 to weave the next four weft strips, tightening the weave as you work.

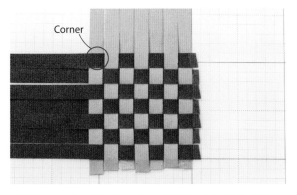

**5.** Weave the final weft strip for this side. The area marked by the red circle will become the corner.

Use double-sided tape to secure the left edge of the first weft strip to prevent the weave from loosening while you work.

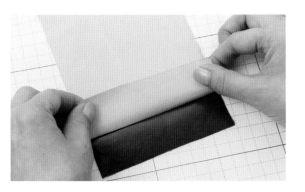

**6.** Cut a piece of self-adhesive fabric double the size of the woven work (refer to your individual project instructions for exact dimensions). This will be the bag's lining. Peel back one edge of the release paper to expose about 2 in (5 cm) of adhesive.

**7.** Align the exposed adhesive with the right edge of the woven work. Peel back half of the release paper to adhere half of the lining to the woven work (leave the release paper in place on the other half). Use your hand to smooth out the lining as you adhere it.

**8.** Completed view of half the lining adhered to the woven work. Fold the other half of the lining back on top of the first half.

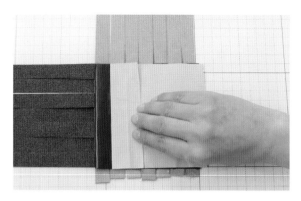

**9.** Next, you'll weave the other side of the bag, adhering the other half of the lining as you work. Start by peeling back the release paper one warp strip width.

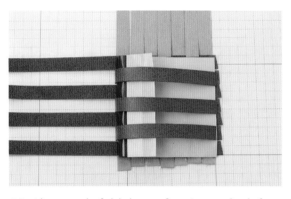

**10.** Alternately fold the weft strips at the left edge of the work.

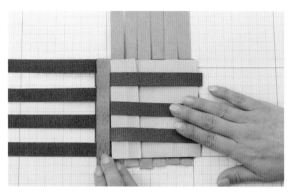

**11.** Fold the leftmost warp strip down over the weft strips folded in step 10.

**12.** Fold the weft strips from step 10 back to the left. Next, peel back the release paper another warp strip width, just like in step 9.

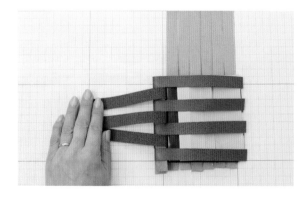

**13.** Now fold the opposite weft strips from step 10 to the right.

**14.** Fold the new leftmost warp strip down over the weft strips folded in step 13.

**15.** Follow this process to continue weaving this side of the bag, peeling back the release paper as you work.

**16.** Completed view. This method produces a three-dimensional bag with one corner and two folded edges.

This method is used to weave the Heart Pochette on page 84. Since the bag is inserted into the metal purse frame, there's no need to finish the edges.

# METHOD #2: WEAVING A LINED BAG WITH AN OPEN TOP AND SIDE

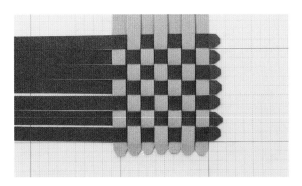

**1.** Follow steps 1–5 on pages 24–25 to construct one side of the bag using the braid weaving technique, but leave the weft (horizontal) strips extending ⅝ in (1.5 cm) beyond the right edge.

Trim corners

**2.** Trim the corners of the strips at an angle as shown.

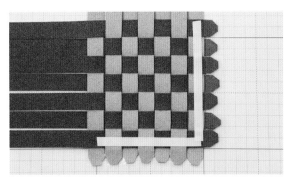

**3.** Adhere double-sided tape to the edges with the extended strips.

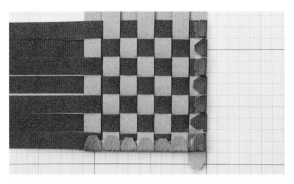

**4.** Fold the trimmed strips and adhere to the double-sided tape to create finished edges.

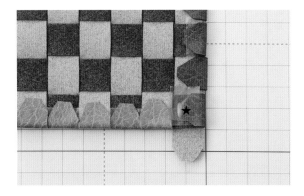

**5.** Use a small piece of double-sided tape on the area marked by a ★ since the warp and weft strips will overlap there.

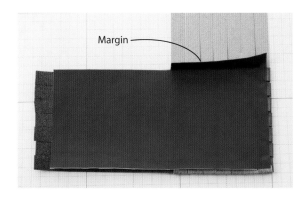

Margin

**6.** Cut a piece of self-adhesive fabric double the size of the woven work, leaving a margin as shown (refer to your individual project instructions for exact dimensions).

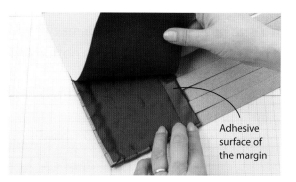

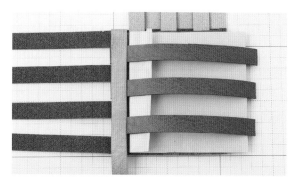

**7.** Follow steps 6 and 7 on page 25 to adhere half of the lining to the woven work. Next, peel back the release paper along the margin to expose the adhesive surface. Fold the other half of the lining back on top of the first, adhering it to the margin.

Adhesive surface of the margin

**8.** Follow steps 9–11 on page 26 to begin weaving the other side of the bag.

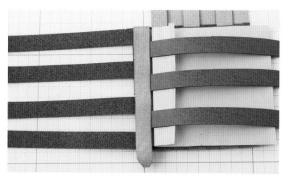

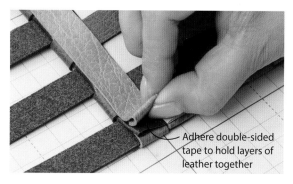

**9.** Trim the folded warp strip so it extends about ⅝ in (1.5 cm) beyond the bottom edge and trim the corners at angles as shown.

**10.** Fold the excess warp strip under and adhere it to the exposed lining.

Adhere double-sided tape to hold layers of leather together

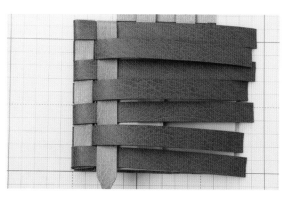

**11.** Follow steps 12–14 on pages 26–27 to weave the second row.

**12.** Repeat steps 9 and 10 above to finish the end of the second folded warp strip.

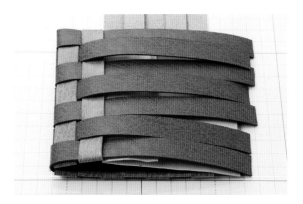

This method is used to weave the Document Folio on page 76. The top and side of the folio need to be open to insert papers, but the edges need to be finished since they'll be visible.

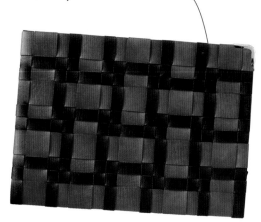

**13.** Follow this process to complete weaving this side of the bag. When you reach the end, repeat steps 9 and 10 on page 29 to finish the weft strips along the right edge.

## METHOD #3: WEAVING A LINED BAG WITH AN OPEN TOP

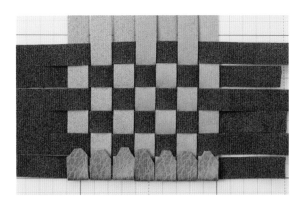

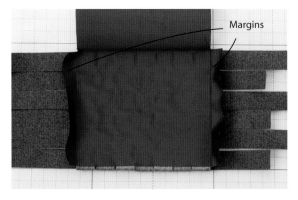

Margins

**1.** Follow steps 1–5 on pages 24–25 to construct one side of the bag using the braid weaving technique, but leave the weft (horizontal) strips extending a couple of inches beyond the left and right edges. Trim the corners of the warp (vertical) strips at an angle along the bottom edge. Adhere double-sided tape and fold the trimmed strips up to create a finished edge.

**2.** Cut a piece of self-adhesive fabric double the size of the woven work, leaving margins along the left and right edges (refer to your individual project instructions for exact dimensions). This will be the lining. Peel back half of the release paper and align with the bottom edge of the woven work. Use your hand to smooth out the lining as you adhere it, removing any air bubbles.

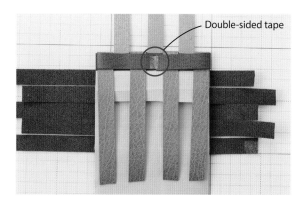

Double-sided tape

**3.** Peel back the release paper along the margins to expose the adhesive surfaces. Fold the other half of the lining back on top of the first, adhering it to the margins. Next, you'll weave the other side of the bag, adhering the other half of the lining as you work.

**4.** Start by peeling back the release paper one weft strip width. Alternately fold the warp strips down at the top edge of the work. Next, fold the first weft strip in (both left and right edges). Use a piece of double-sided tape to hold the weft strip edges together, positioning the seam at a location that will be hidden by a warp strip.

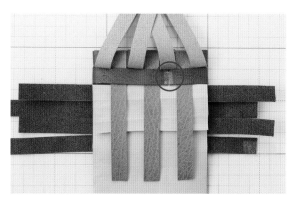

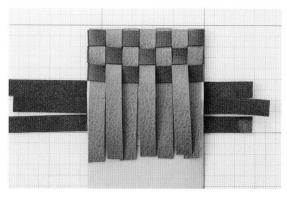

**5.** Fold the warp strips from step 4 back up. Next, peel back the release paper one weft strip width. Now fold the opposite warp strips from step 4 down. Then fold the next weft strip in and secure with tape. Take care to position the seam at a different location than in step 4 so it will be hidden by one of these alternate warp strips.

**6.** Repeat steps 4 and 5 to complete weaving this side of the bag. When you reach the end, follow steps 9 and 10 on page 29 to finish the warp strips along the bottom edge.

This method is used to weave the Slim Clutch on page 63. With this design, the top is open, but the edges are finished.

# METHOD #4: FLAT WEAVING

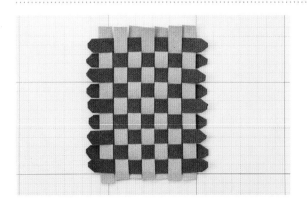

**1.** Follow steps 1–5 on pages 24–25 to work the braid weaving technique, but leave the weft (horizontal) strips extending ⅝ in (1.5 cm) beyond the left and right edges. Trim the corners of the weft strips at an angle as shown.

**2.** Adhere double-sided tape to the edges with the extended strips. Fold the trimmed strips and adhere to the double-sided tape.

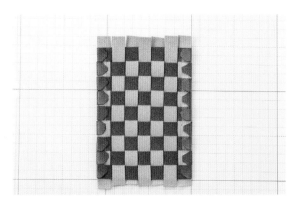

**3.** Completed view of the finished edges created by folding the trimmed weft strips.

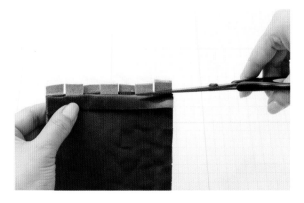

**4.** Cut a piece of self-adhesive fabric the size of the woven work, leaving ⅜ in (1 cm) margins along the top and bottom. Peel back the release paper and adhere it to the wrong side of the work, starting at the center and working outward. Leave the margins unattached. Trim the excess warp strips even with the first weft strip.

**5.** Wrap the margins around the top and bottom edges of the work and adhere to the right side.

**6.** Completed view of a piece of flat weaving with finished edges.

This method is a quick and easy way to finish the edges of simple folders and pouches.

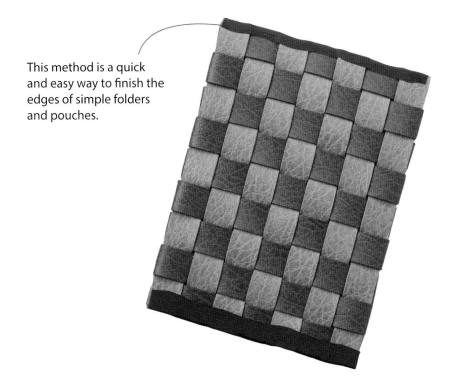

# FINISHING TECHNIQUES

The following guide showcases easy techniques for finishing bags and other small woven goods without the use of a sewing machine. You'll learn how to add a lining, hand stitch seams, and add handles and metal hardware, such as snaps, rivets, and trim. The Colorblock Mini Tote on page 58 is featured as an example, but the same processes are used to finish a variety of projects in this book.

## ADDING A LINING

**1.** Weave the leather strips according to your individual project instructions.

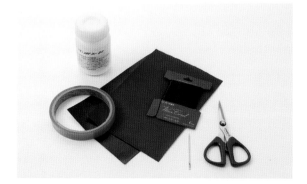

**2.** You'll need self-adhesive fabric for the bag's lining, double-sided tape, scissors, leather glue, a tapestry needle, and waxed cord.

### A NOTE ABOUT SELF-ADHESIVE FABRICS

Self-adhesive fabrics are traditional fabrics coated with a glue-like backing that enables the fabric to adhere to other materials without the need for sewing. This feature makes self-adhesive fabrics ideal for use as linings in woven leather bags.

   The projects in this book use two types of self-adhesive fabrics: leather and satin. Self-adhesive leather can be used to create sturdy, durable linings suitable for bags that will receive a lot of wear and tear. Self-adhesive leather or faux leather is readily available as it is commonly used for upholstery and sporting good repair.

   Self-adhesive satin produces a lighter, more elegant lining suitable for more formal bags. If you can't find self-adhesive satin, just buy regular satin fabric and apply a double-sided adhesive, such as Thermoweb Peel n Stick Fabric Fuse Sheets. Follow the manufacturer's instructions to adhere the double-sided adhesive to satin.

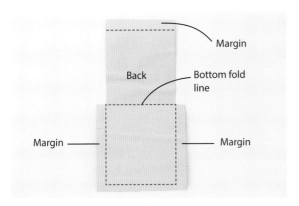

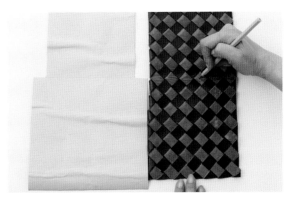

**3.** Cut a piece of self-adhesive fabric for the lining (refer to your individual project instructions for exact dimensions or a template). This lining features ⅜ in (1 cm) wide margins along the top, bottom, and sides for finishing the edges.

**4.** Mark the bottom fold on the wrong side of the woven work to indicate where to align the lining.

Before you adhere the lining, make sure to remove any pieces of tape that were used to temporarily secure the leather strips.

**5.** Peel back one edge of the release paper to expose a bit of the adhesive.

**6.** Adhere the exposed adhesive to the wrong side of the work. Make sure to leave the margins extending beyond the woven work.

**7.** Flip the woven work over so the right side is facing up. Trim the excess self-adhesive fabric at the corners as shown, then wrap the bottom margin only around the edge of the woven work and adhere it to the right side.

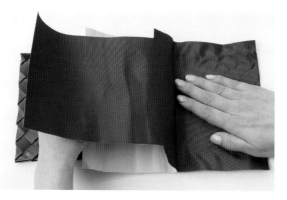

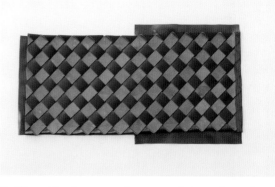

**8.** Flip the work back over. Peel back the rest of the release paper and adhere the rest of the lining to the woven work. Use your hand to smooth out the lining as you adhere it, removing any air bubbles.

**9.** Wrap the top margin around the edge of the woven work and adhere it to the wrong side. This photo shows the right side of the work once the lining has been applied.

**10.** Flip the work back over and fold the side margins in. Use pieces of cellophane tape to temporarily secure the side margins in place. Fold the other half of the bag back on top of the first, adhering to the margins.

**11.** Completed view of the lined bag.

# HAND STITCHING A SEAM

**1.** Thread a tapestry needle with a long piece of waxed cord. Insert the needle through the folded loop closest to the bottom fold of the bag.

**2.** Insert the needle through the corresponding folded loop on the other side of the bag.

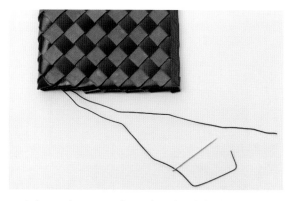

**3.** Adjust the waxed cord so both halves are equal in length.

**4.** Remove the tapestry needle from the waxed cord and tie a square knot.

**5.** Rethread the needle and repeat steps 1 and 2 with the next set of folded loops, then tie a square knot.

**6.** Follow this process to sew the entire side. Trim any excess waxed cord. Apply a dab of glue to the ends and hide them between the woven work and self-adhesive fabric along the top of the bag.

## USING WAXED CORD TO STRAIGHTEN THE WEAVE

Waxed cord can also be used to straighten the weave along an edge. Simply run a piece of waxed cord through the folded loops. This photo shows a nice straight edge along the front of the bag and an uneven weave along the back of the bag where the waxed cord has yet to be inserted.

# INSTALLING METAL HARDWARE

## MAGNETIC SNAPS

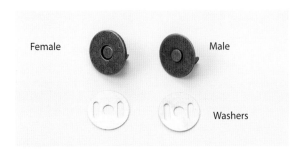

Each magnetic snap has four parts: a female component, a male component, and two washers.

**1.** Position one of the washers in place and cut little slits for the two notches. It may help to mark the notches first before cutting.

**2.** Insert the female component's prongs through the slits from the inside of the bag.

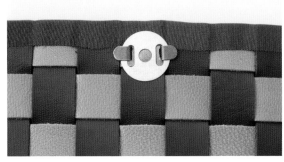

**3.** Thread a washer onto the prongs, then bend the prongs to hold the washer in place.

**4.** Snap the male component to the male component on the inside of the bag. Mark where the prongs align with the bag, then cut slits.

**5.** Insert the prongs through the slits and attach the washer to complete the installation of the magnetic snap.

# RIVETS

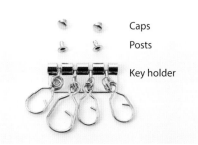

Caps

Posts

Key holder

Rivets are composed of two parts: a cap and a post. Rivets can be used to attach layers of leather together, such as the handle shown on page 59, or to attach other metal components to leather, such as the key holder shown in this example. You will also need a rubber block, leather punch or awl, setting base, rivet setter, and mallet (see page 40).

**1.** Mark the rivet placement. Place the woven work on top of the rubber block. Use a leather punch or awl to punch holes in the marked locations.

**2.** Insert the rivet posts through the holes.

**3.** Place the woven work on top of the setting base. Snap the rivet caps onto the posts (thread the holes of the key holder onto the posts first if using). Position the indented end of the rivet setter on top of the cap. Use a mallet to strike the rivet setter a few times until the rivet is secure.

# SNAP BUTTONS

Snap buttons are composed of four parts: the post, cap, stud, and socket. The post and stud will be set together, while the cap and socket will be set together. Install snap buttons following the same process used to install rivets.

Post

Cap

Stud

Socket

# METAL TRIM

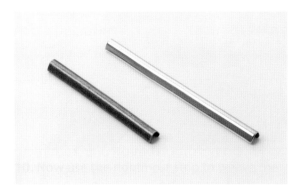

Metal trim can be used to finish the edges of woven leather, providing durability and a professional look.

**1.** Slide the channel on the metal trim onto the edge of the woven leather.

**2.** Cover the metal trim with a scrap of leather to prevent scratches. Use flat-nose pliers to squeeze the metal trim around the leather.

## LEATHERCRAFT TOOLS

You can purchase leather craft tool sets designed specifically for punching holes and installing rivets, snaps, and other fasteners. Look for a set that contains a rubber block, setting base, rivet setter, leather punch, and mallet.

# METAL CLASP

**1.** Weave the leather strips and add a self-adhesive fabric lining according to your individual project instructions. Fold the woven work in half.

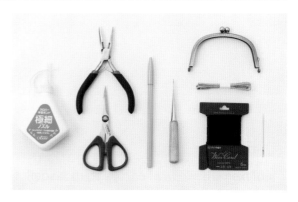

**2.** You'll need craft glue, flat-nose pliers, scissors, a pen, an awl or stiletto, a metal purse clasp, paper twine, waxed cord, and a tapestry needle.

**3.** Place the metal clasp on top of the woven work to decide where to cut. The clasp hinges should align with the folded edges of the woven work.

**4.** Mark the clasp placement on the lining. Also mark the bottom fold of the purse from step 1.

**5.** Position the metal clasp in place on the lining. Trace along the outside edge of the clasp.

**6.** Trim along the marked line.

**7.** Use pieces of double-sided tape to secure the loose ends.

**8.** Insert the trimmed woven work into the metal clasp to check the fit.

**TIP**

If the woven work is too small to fit into the metal clasp, peel back the lining and adjust the weave as necessary. If it's too large, trim the woven work to fit.

**9.** Apply craft glue to the channel on one half of the metal clasp. Use the nozzle of the glue bottle or a chopstick to apply the glue as neatly as possible.

**10.** Cut a piece of paper twine equal in length to the clasp. Untwist the paper twine—this will allow it to absorb more glue and produce a more secure seal.

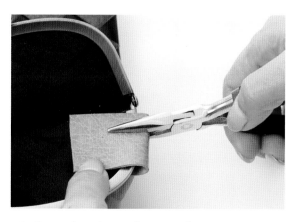

**11.** Insert one side of the woven work into the half of the clasp with glue. Use an awl or stiletto to stuff the paper twine into the channel.

**12.** Once the glue is dry, use pliers to squeeze the clasp just above the hinges. Use a scrap of leather to prevent scratches.

**13.** Repeat steps 9–12 to install the other half of the metal clasp. Use the process shown on pages 36–37 to hand stitch the sides of the purse.

# MAKING LEATHER EMBELLISHMENTS

## TASSELS

**1.** Cut a 3⅛ in (8 cm) long piece of ⅝ in (15 mm) wide leather. Cut to create fringe, leaving ⅜ in (1 cm) of uncut leather along the top.

**2.** Repeat step 1 three more times to create a total of four pieces. Connect the pieces by adhering double-sided tape to the wrong side. Tie a piece of waxed cord into a loop.

**3.** Align the loop with one end of the fringed leather, then roll into a tassel.

**4.** Cut a long piece of waxed cord and fold one end into a loop. Align with the top of the tassel, then wrap the other end of the waxed cord around the loop and the top of the tassel.

**5.** Once the wraps reach the top of the tassel, insert the end of the waxed cord through the loop from step 4.

**6.** Pull the cord end down to hide the loop under the wraps.

**7.** Trim the remaining cord end.

# BRAIDED STRAP

**1.** Cut two slits into a leather strip, leaving a couple inches of uncut leather at each end. The slits should divide the leather strip into thirds. This example uses a ⅝ in (15 mm) wide leather strip.

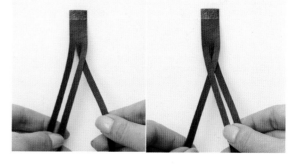

**2.** Tape the end to your work surface. Begin braiding by bringing the rightmost strip over the middle strip, then under the leftmost strip.

**3.** Insert the end of the leather strip into the opening between the leftmost and middle strips.

**4.** Next, you'll insert the end of the leather strip through the opening between the middle and rightmost strips.

**5.** Insert.

**6.** Adjust any twists so the right side of the leather strip is facing up.

**7.** Push the braid up to tighten.

**8.** Repeat steps 2–7 until the braid is complete.

**9.** Completed view of the braided strap.

# PROJECT INSTRUCTIONS

The dimensions provided in the following instructions are general guides. Your results may vary depending on the thickness of your leather or the tightness of your weave. Double-check the size of your woven work and adjust the size of your lining if necessary.

For most projects, the required amounts of leather strips and waxed cord include a bit extra length to accommodate for this variation.

# KEY CADDY

Shown on page 2

## MATERIALS

4½ yd (4 m) of ⅝ in (15 mm)
wide faux leather strips in
chestnut brown

7 x 4⅛ in (18 x 10.5 cm) of
satin self-adhesive fabric
(for lining)

4 x 4 in (10 x 10 cm) of
leather self-adhesive
fabric (for key holder)

11¾ in (30 cm) of dark
brown leather bias tape

39½ in (1 m) of waxed cord

One metal key holder
bracket with rivets

One ring-shaped magnetic
edge clasp

## FINISHED SIZE: 2⅜ x 4¼ in (6 x 11 cm)

## GETTING STARTED

**1.** Cut ten 15¾ in (40 cm) long leather strips.

**2.** Arrange the strips at a 45° angle with the right side facing up.
Secure with cellophane tape.

# INSTRUCTIONS

**1.** Weave 20 rows using the basic weaving technique, until the work measures about 8 in (20 cm) long (see page 22). However, when you fold the leftmost strip, fold it over rather than under, so the wrong side of the leather is visible along the fold.

**2.** Apply the satin self-adhesive fabric to the wrong side of the woven work to create a lining. Trim any excess leather.

**3.** Run waxed cord through the left and right edges to tighten the weave, as shown on page 37.

**4.** Use leather glue to adhere leather bias tape to the top and bottom edges.

**5.** Fold the leather self-adhesive fabric, then attach to the lining witht the key holder bracket rivets, as shown below.

**6.** Use flat-nose pliers to install the magnetic edge clasp on the top edge of the caddy. Use a rivet setter to install the corresponding snap on the right side of the bottom third of the caddy.

**a.** Leave a ⅜ in (1 cm) margin along one edge of the leather self-adhesive fabric. Remove the release paper and fold the remaining portion in half. Fold the margin over and seal in place. The leather should be 1¾ in (4.5 cm) wide.

**b.** Position the leather at the center of the caddy lining. Use a rivet setter to install the metal key holder bracket on top of the leather (refer to page 39).

Snap

Magnetic edge clasp

Leather bias tape adhered in step 4

# CARD CASE

Shown on page 2

Shown on page 2

## MATERIALS

2¾ yd (2.4 m) of ⅝ in
   (15 mm) wide faux leather
   strips in chestnut brown
8¾ x 2½ in (22 x 6.5 cm) of
   satin self-adhesive fabric
39½ in (1 m) of waxed cord
One 2½ in (6.3 cm) metal
   edge trim

**FINISHED SIZE:** 4¼ x 6¾ in (11 x 17 cm)

## GETTING STARTED

**1.** Cut six 15¾ in (40 cm) long leather strips.

**2.** Arrange the strips at a 45° angle with the right side facing up. Secure with cellophane tape.

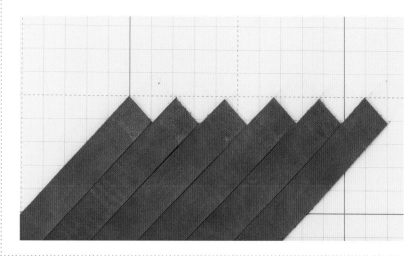

## INSTRUCTIONS

**1.** Weave 24 rows using the basic weaving technique, until the work measures about 9½ in (24 cm) long (see page 22). However, when you fold the leftmost strip, fold it over rather than under, so the wrong side of the leather is visible along the fold.

**2.** Apply the satin self-adhesive fabric to the wrong side of the woven work to create a lining. Trim any excess leather.

**3.** Run waxed cord through both long edges to tighten the weave, as shown on page 37. Fold the woven work in half so it measures 3¼ in (11 cm) long, as shown below. Use waxed cord to hand stitch one long side of the case closed, as shown on page 36.

**4.** Install the metal edge trim, as shown on page 40.

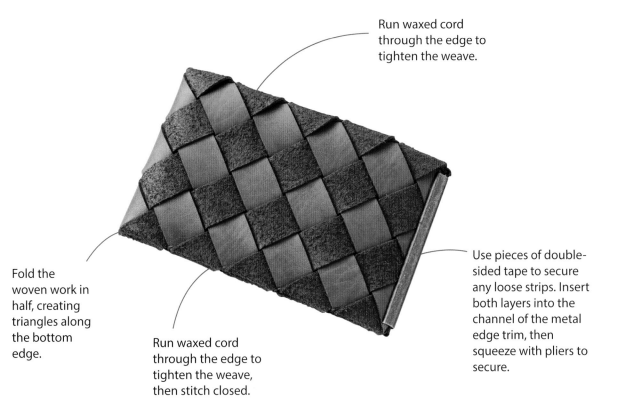

Run waxed cord through the edge to tighten the weave.

Fold the woven work in half, creating triangles along the bottom edge.

Run waxed cord through the edge to tighten the weave, then stitch closed.

Use pieces of double-sided tape to secure any loose strips. Insert both layers into the channel of the metal edge trim, then squeeze with pliers to secure.

# SQUARE TOGGLE POUCHES

Shown on page 3

## MATERIALS

### For the Small Variation

6¾ yd (6.1 m) of ⅝ in
    (15 mm) wide leather
    strips

6¾ x 11¾ in (17 x 30 cm) of
    satin self-adhesive fabric

1½ yd (1.2 m) of waxed cord

### For the Medium Variation

6¼ yd (5.6 m) of 1¼ in
    (30 mm) wide leather
    strips

11¾ in (30 cm) of ⅝ in
    (15 mm) wide faux leather
    strips

8¾ x 15¾ in (22 x 40 cm) of
    satin self-adhesive fabric

1¾ yd (1.5 m) of waxed cord

### For Both Variations

One rivet set

4 in (10 cm) of 1¼ in
    (30 mm) wide leather
    strips

**FINISHED SIZE:** 5¾ x 5¼ in (14.5 x 13.5 cm) for small variation
and 7¼ x 7¼ in (18.5 x 18.5 cm) for medium variation.

## GETTING STARTED

### For the Small Variation

**1.** Cut 17 12½ in (32 cm) long strips of the ⅝ in (15 mm) wide faux
leather. Cut a 13¾ in (35 cm) long strip and set aside for finishing
the pouch opening in step 6.

**2.** Arrange nine warp (vertical) strips with the wrong side facing
up. Weave eight weft (horizontal) strips using the braid weaving
technique to create the first side of the pouch (see step 1 on
page 30).

### For the Medium Variation

**1.** Cut 12 16½ in (42 cm) long strips of the 1¼ in (30 mm) wide
faux leather. Cut a 17¾ in (45 cm) long strip and set aside for
finishing the pouch opening in step 6.

**2.** Arrange six warp (vertical) strips with the wrong side facing
up. Weave six weft (horizontal) strips using the braid weaving
technique to create the first side of the pouch (see step 1 on
page 30).

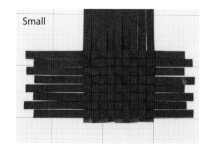

Small

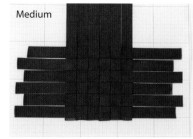

Medium

## INSTRUCTIONS (FOR BOTH VARIATIONS)

**1.** Finish weaving into a bag shape using the braid weaving technique, applying the self-adhesive fabric lining and finishing the ends of the warp strips (see steps 2–6 on pages 30–31).

**2.** Run waxed cord through the sides and bottom of the pouch to straighten the weave, as shown on page 37.

**3.** To make the toggle button: Trim the 4 in (10 cm) long piece of leather into shape.

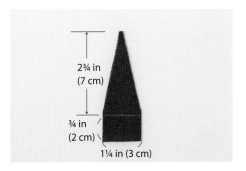

2¾ in (7 cm)

¾ in (2 cm)

1¼ in (3 cm)

**4.** Roll into a button, starting from the wide lower end. Apply a dab of glue to the pointed tip and secure. Use an awl to punch two holes in the button, then thread a piece of waxed cord through the holes.

**5.** Braid three 6 in (15 cm) long waxed cords and fold in half to form the button loop. Attach the button loop to the back of the pouch.

**6.** Wrap the leather strip set aside in step 1 on page 52 around the pouch opening. Glue in place so the ends meet at the side where the handle will be attached.

**7.** Sew the toggle button in place on the front of the pouch.

**8.** Braid an 11¾ in (30 cm) long strip of ⅝ in (15 mm) wide faux leather to create a handle, as shown on page 45. Fold the handle in half and attach to the bag using the rivet (see page 39).

Attach the handle so it covers the seam created in step 6.

Note: This photo shows the Small Variation, but the same techniques apply for the Medium Variation.

# CLASSIC COIN PURSE

Shown on page 4

## MATERIALS

3½ yd (3.2 m) of ⅝ in (15 mm) wide faux leather strips in mahogany or black

4 x 9¾ in (10 x 25 cm) of satin self-adhesive fabric

One 2 x 4 in (5 x 10 cm) round metal purse clasp with wooden baubles

20 in (50 cm) of waxed cord in mahogany or black

## FINISHED SIZE: 4 x 4¼ in (10 x 11 cm)

## GETTING STARTED

**1.** Cut eight 15¾ in (40 cm) long strips of leather strips.

**2.** Arrange the strips at a 45° angle with the right side facing up. Secure with cellophane tape.

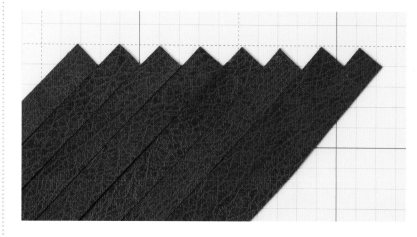

## INSTRUCTIONS

**1.** Weave 25 rows using the basic weaving technique (see page 22). Work on top of a sheet of graph paper to ensure that the work measures 4 in (10 cm) wide, so it will fit into the metal purse clasp.

**2.** Apply satin self-adhesive fabric to the wrong side of the woven work to create a lining.

**3.** Install the metal purse clasp, as shown on page 41.

**4.** To complete the purse, use waxed cord to hand stitch the sides, as shown on page 36.

## VARIATION

These instructions can also be used to create a longer case suitable for storing eyeglasses. Simply cut eight 25½ in (65 cm) long strips, then weave until the work measures 15¾ in (40 cm) long.

This longer style case is featured in the guide on page 41.

# KISS CLASP POCHETTE

Shown on page 5

## MATERIALS

6¾ yd (6 m) of ⅝ in (15 mm)
wide faux leather strips in
light brown

7 yd (6.25 m) of ⅝ in (15 mm)
wide faux leather strips in
dark brown

6 x 23¾ in (15 x 60 cm) of
satin self-adhesive fabric

One 6⅛ x 1 in (15.5 x 2.5 cm)
rectangular metal purse
clasp with baubles

2¼ yd (2 m) of waxed cord
in dark brown

One 47 in (120 cm) purse
chain with swivel hooks

**FINISHED SIZE:** 6 x 10¼ in (15 x 26 cm)

## GETTING STARTED

**1.** Cut six 39½ in (100 cm) long strips of each color of leather.
You'll use the leftover dark brown leather to make a tassel.

**2.** Arrange the strips at a 45° angle in the following order: three
light brown strips with the right side facing up, six dark brown
strips with the wrong side facing up, and then three more
light brown strips with the right side facing up. Secure with
cellophane tape.

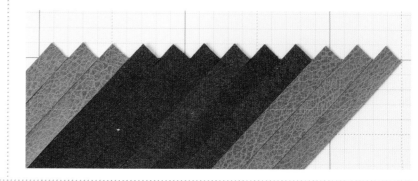

# INSTRUCTIONS

**1.** Weave 55 rows using the basic weaving technique, until the work measures about 21¾ in (55 cm) long (see page 22). Work on top of a sheet of graph paper to ensure that the work measures 6⅛ in (15.5 cm) wide so it will fit into the metal purse clasp.

**2.** Apply satin self-adhesive fabric to the wrong side of the woven work to create a lining.

**3.** Install the metal purse clasp, as shown on page 41.

**4.** Use waxed cord to hand stitch the sides of the purse, as shown on page 36.

**5.** Make the tassel, as shown on page 44. Attach it to one of the swivel hooks on the purse chain.

Thread the tassel's loop onto the swivel hook, then clip the chain to the loops on the metal purse clasp.

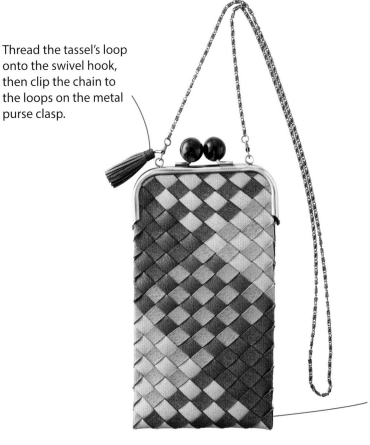

Refer to page 36 for detailed instructions on hand stitching the sides of the purse using waxed cord.

# COLORBLOCK MINI TOTE

Shown on page 6

## MATERIALS

10 yd (9 m) of ⅝ in (15 mm)
   wide faux leather strips
7 x 15 in (18 x 38 cm) of
   satin self-adhesive fabric
1¾ yd (1.6 m) of waxed cord
Two sets of rivets

## NOTE

Genuine leather tends to
be thicker than faux leather
and results in a stiffer
woven bag. Keep in mind
that the row counts listed
in these instructions may
differ based on the type of
leather used.

**FINISHED SIZE:** 5¾ x 6¼ in (14.5 x 16 cm)

## GETTING STARTED

**1.** Cut 12 25½ in (65 cm) long leather strips.

**2.** Arrange the strips at a 45° angle with the right side facing up.
Secure with cellophane tape.

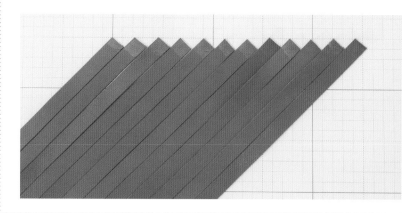

# INSTRUCTIONS

**1.** Weave 32 rows using the basic weaving technique, until the work measures about 13¾ in (35 cm) long (see page 22).

**2.** Refer to the guide on pages 34–37 to attach the lining and hand stitch the sides of the bag.

**3.** Cut two 11¾ in (30 cm) long leather strips for the handles, a length of leather equal to the circumference of the bag opening to be used for the binding, and two ¾ in (2 cm) triangles of leather for each handle decoration (four total).

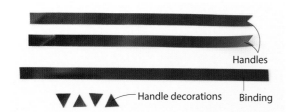

Handles

Handle decorations    Binding

**4.** Use double-sided tape to temporarily secure one end of each handle to the self-adhesive fabric along the top edge of the bag. Note how the handles are attached to opposite sides of the bag.

**5.** Glue the binding cut in step 3 to the self-adhesive fabric around the bag opening. Align the ends of the binding so they will be hidden by the handle.

**6.** Align the unattached end of the handle to cover the ends of binding. Layer the two triangles on top to create a star shape.

**7.** Fasten the decorative star and handle in place using a rivet (refer to page 39). Follow the same process to finish attaching the handle on the other side of the bag.

# BOW CLUTCH

Shown on page 7

## MATERIALS

### For the Single Color Variation

19 yd (17 m) of ⅝ in (15 mm) wide leather strips

1¼ yd (1 m) of 1¼ in (30 mm) wide leather strips

1¾ yd (1.4 m) of waxed cord

### For the Two Color Variation

6 yd (5.5 m) of ⅝ in (15 mm) wide faux leather strips in light brown

12 yd (11 m) of ⅝ in (15 mm) wide faux leather strips in dark brown

1¼ yd (1 m) of 1¼ in (30 mm) wide faux leather strips in dark brown

1¾ yd (1.4 m) of waxed cord in dark brown

### For Both Variations

12¾ x 17¾ in (32 x 45 cm) of satin self-adhesive fabric

One magnetic snap set

## FINISHED SIZE: 11 x 8 in (28 x 20 cm)

## GETTING STARTED

**1.** Cut 18 19¾ in (50 cm) long warp (vertical) strips and 12 24½ in (62 cm) long weft (horizontal) strips of the ⅝ in (15 mm) wide leather. For the Two Color Variation, cut six light brown warp strips and 12 dark brown warp strips, plus four light brown weft strips, and eight dark brown weft strips.

**2.** Arrange the 18 warp strips with the wrong side facing up. For the Two Color Variation, position a light brown leather strip between two dark brown leather strips, then repeat five more times. Weave the 12 weft strips using the braid weaving technique to create the first side of the clutch (see step 1 on page 30).

## INSTRUCTIONS

**1.** Finish weaving into a bag shape using the braid weaving technique, applying the self-adhesive fabric lining and finishing the ends of the warp strips (see steps 2–6 on pages 30–31).

**2.** Run waxed cord through each opening edge and the other three sides of the clutch to straighten the weave, as shown on page 37.

**3.** Install the magnetic snap, as shown on page 38. Position the snap between the two top rows of weaving.

**4.** Cut a 23¾ in (60 cm) long piece of 1¼ in (30 mm) wide leather. This trim will be used to hide the magnetic snap components and finish the opening edges of the clutch.

**5.** Wrap the trim around the clutch opening so the ends meet on top of one of the magnetic snap components. Glue the trim in place, leaving the area over the magnetic snap unattached. Cut a 2½ in (6 cm) long piece of leather and insert it between the woven clutch and unattached trim. This will be the middle strap of the bow. Adhere a small piece of double-sided tape to the end of the middle strap.

**6.** Cut a 9½ in (24 cm) long piece of leather for the bow. Fold into a loop and adhere a small piece of double-sided tape to hold the ends together. Align the loop on top of the trim, matching up the seams.

**7.** Remove the paper backings on the double-sided tape. Wrap the middle strap around the loop and the unattached trim, hiding the end between the trim and woven clutch. If necessary, use another piece of double-sided tape or glue to adhere the unattached trim to the woven clutch.

Double-sided tape

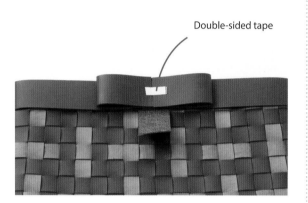

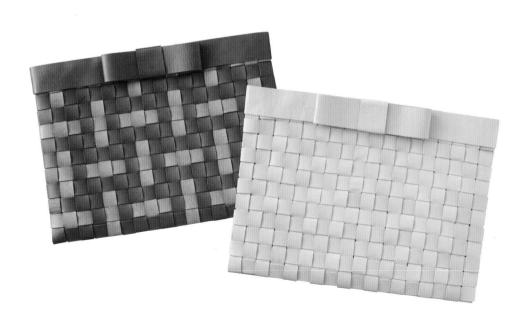

# SLIM CLUTCH

Shown on page 8

## MATERIALS

Color A: 5½ yd (5 m) of
⅝ in (15 mm) wide leather
strips in white or navy
blue

Color B: 5½ yd (5 m) of
⅝ in (15 mm) wide leather
strips in green or silver

11¾ x 11¾ in (30 x 30 cm) of
satin self-adhesive fabric

1½ yd (1.2 m) of waxed cord

One magnetic snap set

3⅛ x 1⅜ in (8 x 3.5 cm) scrap
of leather (for magnetic
snap support)

One decorative metal
button

## FINISHED SIZE: 9¾ x 5½ in (25 x 14 cm)

## GETTING STARTED

**1.** Cut eight 13¾ in (35 cm) long warp (vertical) strips and four
21¾ in (55 cm) long weft (horizontal) strips of each color of
leather.

**2.** Arrange the 16 warp strips with the wrong side facing up. Start
and end with one strip of Color A, alternating two strips of Color
B, then two strips of Color A in between.

**3.** Use the braid weaving technique to create the first side of the
clutch (see step 1 on page 30). Use Color A for the first weft strip,
then alternate two strips of Color B, two strips of Color A, two
strips of Color B, and finish with one strip of Color A.

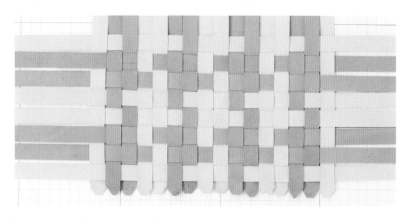

## INSTRUCTIONS

**1.** Finish weaving into a bag shape using the braid weaving technique, applying the self-adhesive fabric lining and finishing the ends of the warp strips (see steps 2–6 on pages 30–31).

**2.** Run waxed cord through each opening edge and the other three sides of the clutch to straighten the weave, as shown on page 37.

**3.** Install the magnetic snap (refer to page 38): Install the female component of the magnetic snap on the scrap of leather, then glue it to the lining at the center back of the clutch. Install the male component of the magnetic snap in the corresponding spot on the lining at the center front of the clutch. Sew the metal button to the outside of the clutch to cover the magnetic snap.

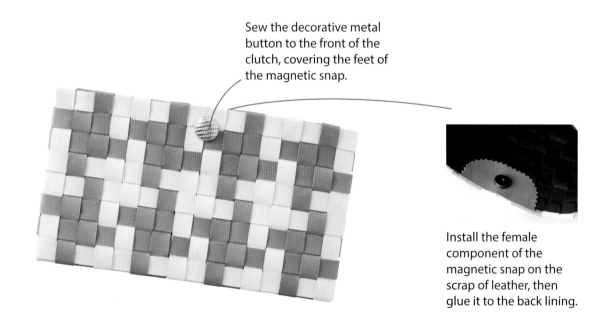

Sew the decorative metal button to the front of the clutch, covering the feet of the magnetic snap.

Install the female component of the magnetic snap on the scrap of leather, then glue it to the back lining.

# TABLET CASE

Shown on page 8

## MATERIALS

Color A: 6¼ yd (5.7 m) of
⅝ in (15 mm) wide leather
strips in green or navy
blue

Color B: 6¼ yd (5.7 m) of
⅝ in (15 mm) wide leather
strips in white or silver

6¾ x 15¾ in (17 x 40 cm) of
satin self-adhesive fabric

1½ yd (1.4 m) of waxed cord

21¼ in (54 cm) of ⅝ in
(15 mm) wide leather
strips in Color B (for belt-
style closure)

⅝ in (15 mm) wide metal
belt buckle

Two 1¼ in (30 mm) metal
corners

## FINISHED SIZE: 6 x 8¾ in (15 x 22 cm)

## GETTING STARTED

**1.** Cut seven 19¾ in (50 cm) long warp (vertical) strips and five
13¾ in (55 cm) long weft (horizontal) strips of each color of
leather.

**2.** Arrange the 14 warp strips with the wrong side facing up. Start
with the seven strips of Color A, then finish with the seven strips
of Color B.

**3.** Use the braid weaving technique to create the first side of the
clutch (see step 1 on page 28). Use Color A for the first five weft
strips, then use Color B for the final five weft strips.

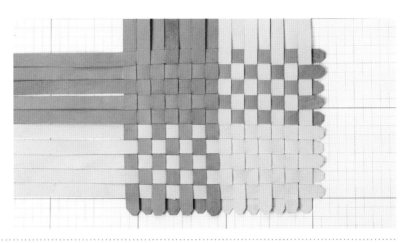

# INSTRUCTIONS

**1.** Finish the ends of the warp strips along the bottom and the ends of the weft strips along the right edge, then apply half of the self-adhesive fabric lining (see steps 2–7 on pages 28–29).

**2.** Finish weaving into a bag shape using the braid weaving technique, applying the other half of the self-adhesive fabric lining and finishing the ends of the warp and weft strips (see steps 8–13 on pages 29–30).

**3.** Run waxed cord through each opening edge and the other two sides of the clutch to straighten the weave, as shown on page 37.

**4.** Install the metal corners, as shown below.

**5.** Make the belt-style closure, as shown below.

Apply glue to the channels of the metal corners, then adhere to the corners of the case.

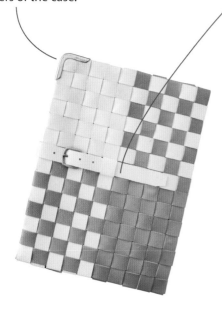

**a.** Thread a 19¾ in (50 cm) long piece of leather onto the buckle. Fold the end over ⅝ in (15 mm). Punch the prong through the folded leather, then glue to secure the buckle in place.

**b.** Use the remaining 1½ in (4 cm) piece of leather to make a belt loop. Thread the loop onto the belt.

**c.** Trim the other end of the belt into a point. Position the buckle on the front of case, then wrap the belt around the spine and bring the pointed end to the front again, inserting it under a couple woven strips as you wrap in order to secure it to the case.

**d.** Use an awl to punch a few holes in the pointed end of the belt.

# GUSSETED MINI PURSE

Shown on page 10

## MATERIALS

6¾ yd (6 m) of ¼ in (5 mm) wide suede cord in brown

6¾ yd (6 m) of ¼ in (5 mm) wide suede cord in yellow

8 x 6¾ in (20 x 17 cm) of satin self-adhesive fabric

10 x 6 in (25.5 x 15 cm) of self-adhesive felt

One 3½ x 2¼ in (9 x 5.5 cm) rectangular metal purse clasp with triangular gussets

## NOTE

These instructions are for the brown and yellow color variation. Refer to page 98 for more information on the materials and starting arrangements necessary to create the other color variations shown on page 10. The rest of the instructions are the same for all color variations.

## FINISHED SIZE: 3¾ x 3 x 1¾ in (9.5 x 7.5 x 4.5 cm)

## GETTING STARTED

**1.** Cut ten 19¾ in (50 cm) long strips of each color of suede cord.

**2.** Arrange the strips at a 45° angle with the right side facing up, alternating brown and yellow strips. Secure with cellophane tape.

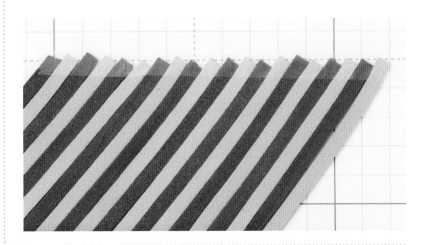

# INSTRUCTIONS

**1.** Weave using the basic weaving technique, until the work measures about 9¾ in (25 cm) long (see page 22). Work on top of a sheet of graph paper to ensure that the work measures 3½ in (9 cm) wide so it will fit into the metal purse clasp.

**2.** Make a template for the purse outside (see page 71). Use the template to cut the woven work to size. Before you cut the woven work, apply masking tape along the cutting lines to prevent the work from unraveling.

**3.** Make templates and cut the remaining purse pieces out (see pages 71–72 for templates).

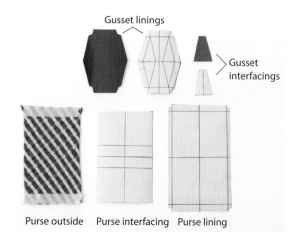

Gusset linings

Gusset interfacings

Purse outside    Purse interfacing    Purse lining

| Piece | Quantity | Material |
|---|---|---|
| Gusset linings | 2 | Satin self-adhesive fabric |
| Gusset interfacings | 2 | Self-adhesive felt |
| Purse outside | 1 | Woven work (cut in step 2) |
| Purse interfacing | 1 | Self-adhesive felt |
| Purse lining | 1 | Satin self-adhesive fabric |

**4.** Peel half of the release paper off the purse lining. With the felt side down, align the center of purse interfacing with the center of the purse lining. Press down to adhere.

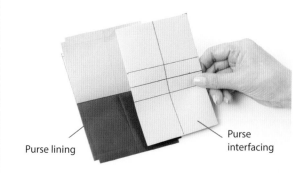

Purse lining

Purse interfacing

**5.** Remove the rest of the release paper and adhere the rest of the interfacing to the lining. Completed view of step 4 with the paper side of the felt facing up.

**6.** Peel the release paper off the purse interfacing. Fold the margins in along the long edges of the lining and adhere to the purse interfacing.

**7.** Adhere the wrong side of the woven purse outside to the purse interfacing.

**8.** Remove the masking tape from the purse outside. Fold the margins along the short edges of the lining and adhere to the right side of the purse outside. The main part of the purse is now complete.

**9.** Peel half of the release paper off one gusset lining. With the felt side down, adhere one gusset interfacing to the gusset lining as shown.

**10.** Remove the rest of the release paper and fold the gusset lining in half as shown. Repeat steps 9 and 10 with the remaining gusset lining and gusset interfacing.

**11.** Adhere pieces of double-sided tape to the purse lining as shown.

**12.** Remove the release paper from the double-sided tape. Adhere the gusset lining margins to the tape, folding the purse into shape.

**13.** This bag requires a metal purse clasp with triangular gussets, which allow the mouth of the purse to open wider than the bottom.

**14.** Apply glue to the top channels of the clasp and insert the opening edges of the purse. The clasp will not be attached along the sides, but will sit inside the gussets.

**15.** Make a handle: Cut a piece of suede cord to desired length. Thread the ends through the loops of the metal purse clasp, then fold and glue in place.

# FULL-SIZE TEMPLATES: GUSSETED MINI PURSE

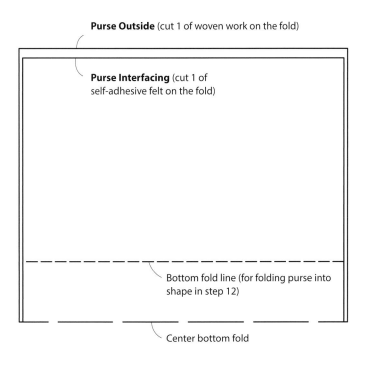

**Purse Outside** (cut 1 of woven work on the fold)

**Purse Interfacing** (cut 1 of self-adhesive felt on the fold)

Bottom fold line (for folding purse into shape in step 12)

Center bottom fold

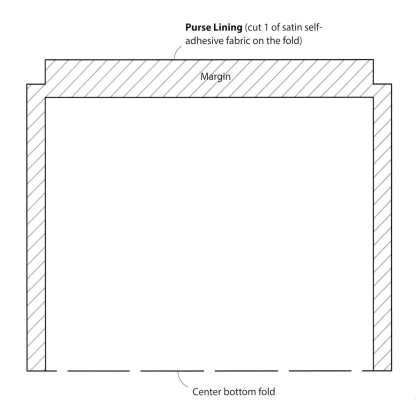

**Purse Lining** (cut 1 of satin self-adhesive fabric on the fold)

Margin

Center bottom fold

# FULL-SIZE TEMPLATES: GUSSETED MINI PURSE

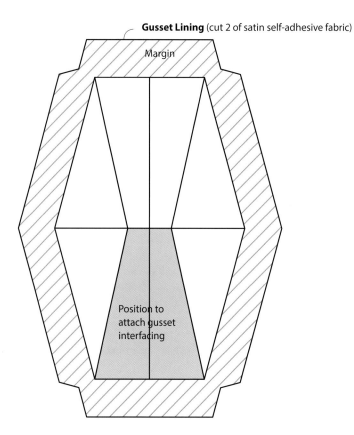

**Gusset Lining** (cut 2 of satin self-adhesive fabric)

Margin

Position to attach gusset interfacing

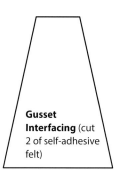

**Gusset Interfacing** (cut 2 of self-adhesive felt)

# TEXTURED SLOUCH BAG

Shown on page 11

## MATERIALS

22 yd (20 m) of ⅝ in
(15 mm) leather strips in
black, camel, or purple

2¼ yd (2 m) of waxed cord
in black, camel, or purple

11½ x 12¾ in (29 x 32 cm)
of leather self-adhesive
fabric

One 6 in (15 cm) horseshoe-
shaped metal purse frame
with removable bars

## NOTE

Look for soft, thin leather
to achieve the slouchy look
characteristic of this bag
design.

**FINISHED SIZE:** 9½ x 8 in (24 x 20 cm)

## GETTING STARTED

**1.** Cut 22 35½ in (90 cm) long leather strips.

**2.** Arrange the strips at a 45° angle with the right side facing up.
Secure with cellophane tape.

## INSTRUCTIONS

**1.** Weave using the basic weaving technique, until the work measures about 19¾ in (50 cm) long (see page 22).

**2.** Cut a piece of leather self-adhesive fabric according to the dimensions listed in the step 4 diagram below.

**3.** Remove the release paper and adhere to the wrong side of the woven work (leave the release paper in place on the margins).

**4.** Fold the short edges of the woven work over 2–2¾ in (5–7 cm) and adhere the leather self-adhesive fabric to the right side of the woven work, overlapping at least 1¼ in (3 cm). This will create casings for the bars of the metal purse clasp.

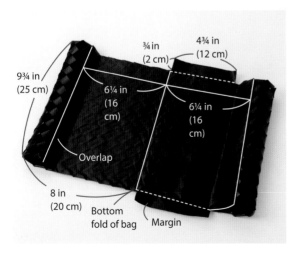

**5.** You'll need a horseshoe-shaped metal purse clasp with removable horizontal bars.

Bar

**6.** Unscrew one of the bars and insert it through one of the casings created in step 4. Screw the bar back in place on the metal purse clasp (if desired, used glue to permanently secure the bar in place).

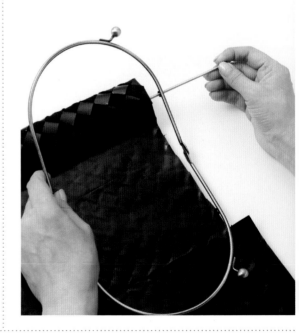

**7.** Adjust the woven work to create the gathers along the bar.

**8.** Repeat steps 6 and 7 to install the other bar along the other casing. Remove the release paper, fold the margins in, and fold the bag in half, adhering the margins to the lining (refer to step 10 on page 36).

**9.** Use waxed cord to hand stitch the sides of the bag, as shown on page 36.

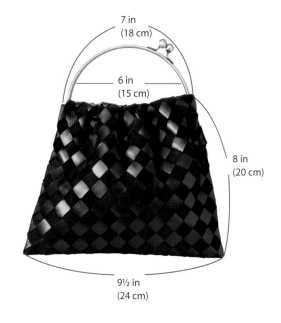

7 in
(18 cm)

6 in
(15 cm)

8 in
(20 cm)

9½ in
(24 cm)

# DOCUMENT FOLIO

Shown on page 12

## MATERIALS

10 yd (9.2 m) of ⅝ in (15 mm)
   wide faux leather strips in
   black

6 yd (5.3 m) of 1¼ in (30 mm)
   wide faux leather strips in
   brown

13 x 17¾ in (33 x 45 cm) of
   satin self-adhesive fabric

2 yd (1.8 m) of waxed cord
   in brown

Two 1¼ in (30 mm) metal
   corners

## FINISHED SIZE: 12¼ x 8¾ in (31 x 22 cm)

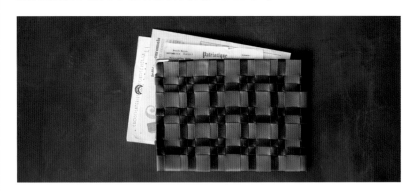

## GETTING STARTED

**1.** Cut ten 19¾ in (50 cm) long warp (vertical) strips and six
27½ in (70 cm) long weft (horizontal) strips of black. Cut five
19¾ in (50 cm) long warp (vertical) strips and four 27½ in (70 cm)
long weft (horizontal) strips of brown.

**2.** Arrange the 15 warp strips with the wrong side facing up. Start
and end with one strip of black, alternating one strip of brown
and two strips of black in between.

**3.** Use the braid weaving technique to create the first side of the
folio (see step 1 on page 28). Use brown for the first weft strip,
then alternate two strips of black and one strip of brown three
times, until ten rows are complete.

# INSTRUCTIONS

**1.** Finish the ends of the warp strips along the bottom and the ends of the weft strips along the right edge, then apply half of the self-adhesive fabric lining (see steps 2–7 on pages 28–29).

**2.** Finish weaving into a bag shape using the braid weaving technique, applying the other half of the self-adhesive fabric lining and finishing the ends of the warp and weft strips (see steps 8–13 on pages 29–30).

**3.** Run waxed cord through each opening edge and the other two sides of the folio to straighten the weave, as shown on page 37.

**4.** Install the metal corners, as shown below.

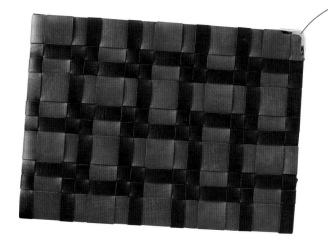

Apply glue to the channels of the metal corners, then adhere to the corners of the folio. If necessary, trim the corners of the woven work before installing the metal corners.

# EYEGLASS CASE

Shown on page 13

## MATERIALS

6¼ yd (5.6 m) of ⅝ in
(15 mm) faux leather
strips in light brown

6¼ yd (5.6 m) of ⅝ in
(15 mm) faux leather
strips in dark brown

9½ x 11¾ in (24 x 30 cm) of
satin self-adhesive fabric

23¾ in (60 cm) of dark
brown leather bias tape

4½ yd (4 m) of waxed cord
in dark brown

1¼ in (3 cm) scrap of leather
(for button)

One rivet set

## FINISHED SIZE: 8 x 3⅛ in (20 x 8 cm)

## GETTING STARTED

**1.** Cut eight 27½ in (70 cm) long strips of each color of leather.

**2.** Arrange the strips at a 45° angle with the right side facing up, alternating dark brown and light brown strips. Secure with cellophane tape.

**3.** Weave 32 rows using the basic weaving technique, until the work measures about 11¾ in (30 cm) long (see page 22).

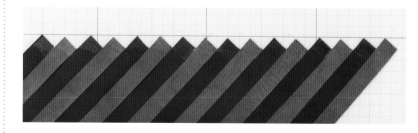

# INSTRUCTIONS

**1.** Using the template on page 81, cut a lining of satin self-adhesive fabric. Adhere the lining to the wrong side of the woven work, peeling the release paper off the satin self-adhesive fabric as you work.

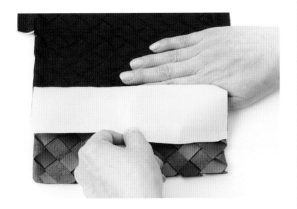

**2.** Use the template on page 81 to trim the woven work into shape along the curved edges only, as shown on page 41. Use pieces of double-sided tape to secure loose ends (refer to step 7 on page 42).

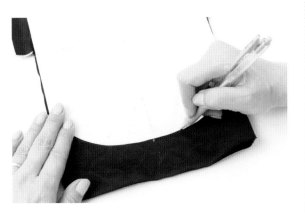

**3.** Use leather glue to adhere leather bias tape to the curved edges.

**4.** View of the right side after the bias tape has been applied to the curved edges.

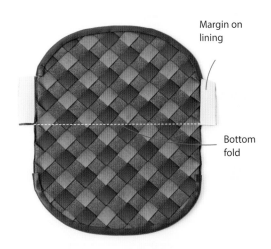

Margin on lining

Bottom fold

**5.** Cut a circle out of the leather scrap and punch a hole at the center. Install the rivet with the leather circle sandwiched in between (refer to page 39).

**6.** Remove the release paper, fold the margins in, and fold the case in half, adhering the margins to the lining (refer to step 10 on page 36). Next, use waxed cord to hand stitch the sides of the case, as shown on page 36.

**7.** Cut three 39½ in (1 m) long pieces of waxed cord. Braid the waxed cords and knot the ends. Wrap the braided cord around the case and button to keep the case closed.

Braided cord

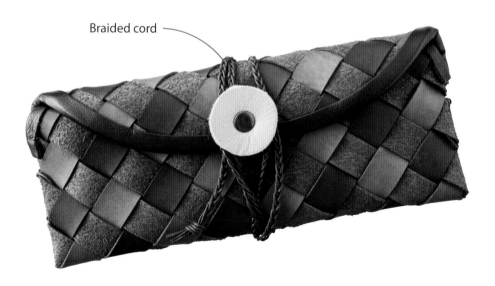

# FULL-SIZE TEMPLATE: EYEGLASS CASE

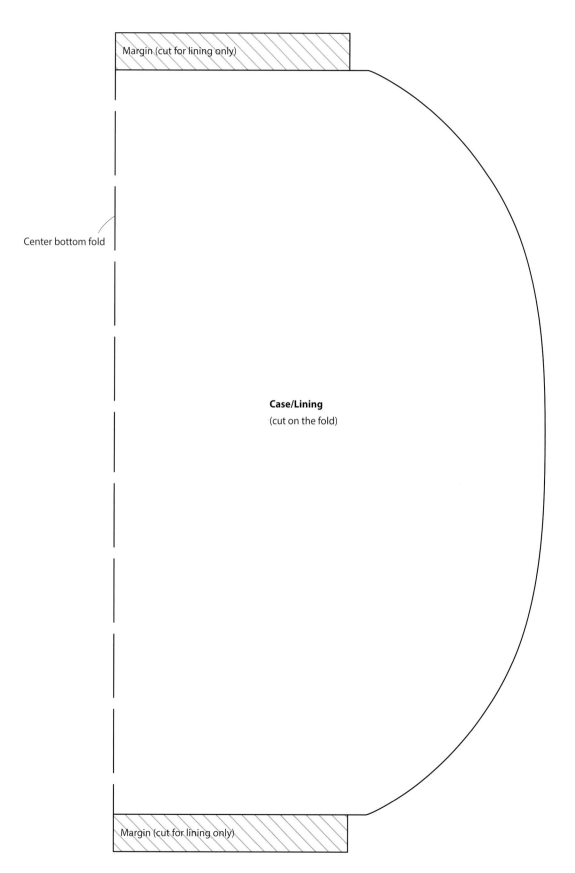

Margin (cut for lining only)

Center bottom fold

**Case/Lining**
(cut on the fold)

Margin (cut for lining only)

# ENVELOPE CLUTCH

Shown on page 14

## MATERIALS

19 yd (17 m) of ⅝ in (15 mm)
  wide leather strips in
  metallic silver
11½ x 17¾ in (29 x 45 cm) of
  satin self-adhesive fabric
31½ in (80 cm) of faux
  leather bias tape in pink
One magnetic snap set
2¼ yd (2 m) of waxed cord
2 in (5 cm) square scrap of
  leather (for tassel)
4 in (10 cm) square scrap of
  leather (for magnetic snap
  support)

## FINISHED SIZE: 9½ x 6¼ in (24 x 16 cm)

## GETTING STARTED

**1.** Cut 21 31½ in (80 cm) long leather strips.

**2.** Arrange the strips at a 45° angle with the right side facing up.
Secure with cellophane tape.

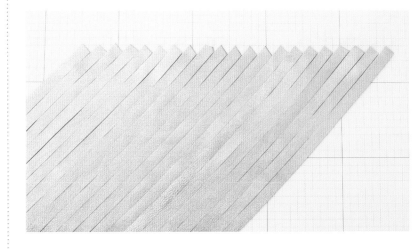

# INSTRUCTIONS

**1.** Weave 50 rows using the basic weaving technique (see page 22).

**2.** Trim the top 5½ in (14 cm) into a point to create the flap. Use pieces of double-sided tape to secure the loose ends (refer to step 7 on page 42).

**3.** Using the woven work as a template, cut a self-adhesive fabric lining with ¾ in (2 cm) margins along the middle section, as shown below. Apply the self-adhesive fabric lining to the wrong side of the woven work.

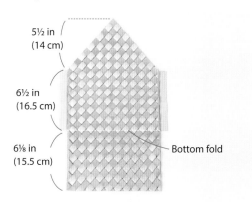

5½ in (14 cm)

6½ in (16.5 cm)

6⅛ in (15.5 cm)

Bottom fold

**4.** Install the magnetic snap (refer to page 38): Install the male component of the magnetic snap on the 4 in (10 cm) square scrap of leather, then glue it to the lining at the point of the flap. Fold the clutch into shape and install the female component of the magnetic snap in the corresponding spot on the outside of the clutch.

**5.** Next, unfold the clutch and use leather glue to adhere leather bias tape to the edges of the flap and clutch opening, as shown below.

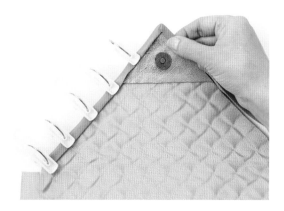

**6.** With the lining facing up, fold the margins in, then fold the bottom portion of the clutch up, adhering it to the margins (refer to step 10 on page 36). Use waxed cord to hand stitch the sides of the clutch, as shown on page 36.

**7.** Make the tassel (see page 44). Attach it to the flap on the outside of the clutch.

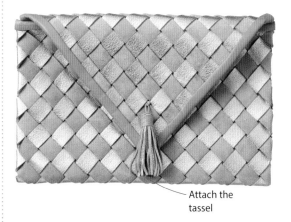

Attach the tassel

# HEART POCHETTE

Shown on page 15

## MATERIALS

6¾ yd (6 m) of ⅝ in (15 mm) wide leather strips in metallic bronze or pink

7 x 13 in (18 x 33 cm) of satin self-adhesive fabric

19¾ in (50 cm) of waxed cord

One 7 in (18 cm) double curve metal purse clasp with handle loops

One metal purse chain with swivel hooks (15 in [38 cm] and 47¼ in [120 cm] chains were used for the samples featured on pages 85 and 15)

## NOTE

The number of weft strips needed to measure 6⅛ in (15.5 cm) may vary based on the thickness of your leather. You will most likely need to weave 9 or 10 weft strips.

## FINISHED SIZE: 7 x 6 in (18 x 15 cm)

## GETTING STARTED

**1.** Cut ten 11¾ in (30 cm) long warp (vertical) strips and nine 12¾ in (32 cm) long weft (horizontal) strips of leather.

**2.** Arrange the 10 warp strips with the wrong side facing up. Weave the nine weft strips using the braid weaving technique to create the first side of the pochette (see steps 1–5 on pages 24–25).

**3.** Adjust the woven work so the bottom and right edges measure 6⅛ in (15.5 cm).

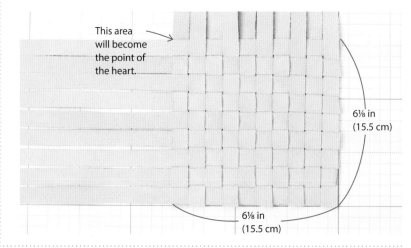

This area will become the point of the heart.

6⅛ in (15.5 cm)

6⅛ in (15.5 cm)

## INSTRUCTIONS

**1.** Finish weaving into a bag shape using the braid weaving technique, applying the self-adhesive fabric lining (see steps 6–16 on pages 25–27).

**2.** Run waxed cord through the two folded sides of the pochette to straighten the weave, as shown on page 37.

**3.** Trace the outline of the metal purse clasp, then cut along the marked lines to trim the woven work into shape. The corner of the woven work will become the bottom point of the heart. Install the metal purse clasp, as shown on page 41.

**4.** Use the swivel hooks to clip the purse chain to the loops on the purse clasp.

Clip the chain to the purse clasp.

# CLASSIC CAT PURSE

Shown on page 16

## MATERIALS

8¼ yd (7.5 m) of 1¼ in (30 mm) wide faux leather strips in brown or black

10¼ x 23¾ in (36 x 60 cm) of satin self-adhesive fabric

3⅛ x 5⅛ in (8 x 13 cm) of self-adhesive felt or card stock

One 6 x 3½ in (15 x 9 cm) rectangular metal purse frame with bars and handle loops

One 15¾ in (40 cm) metal purse chain with swivel hooks

**FINISHED SIZE:** 5⅛ x 5½ x 3¼ in (13 x 14 x 8.5 cm)

## GETTING STARTED

**1.** Cut two 37½ in (95 cm) long and eight 27½ in (70 cm) long leather strips.

**2.** Mark a 6 in (15 cm) square on a sheet of graph paper.

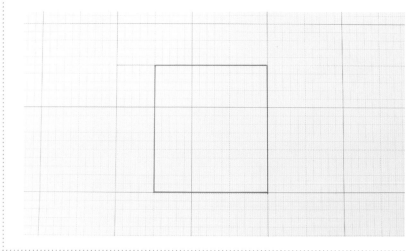

**3.** Arrange five warp strips with the wrong side facing up: Start with two 27½ in (70 cm) long strips, then one 37½ in (95 cm) long strip, then finish with two more 27½ in (70 cm) long strips. Secure with cellophane tape just below the marked square.

**4.** Use the braid weaving technique to fill the marked square. Use 27½ in (70 cm) long strips for the first two weft strips, then the remaining 37½ in (95 cm) long strip, then finish with two more 27½ in (70 cm) long strips.

**5.** Adjust the woven work so the ends of the leather strips extend beyond the marked square, as noted below.

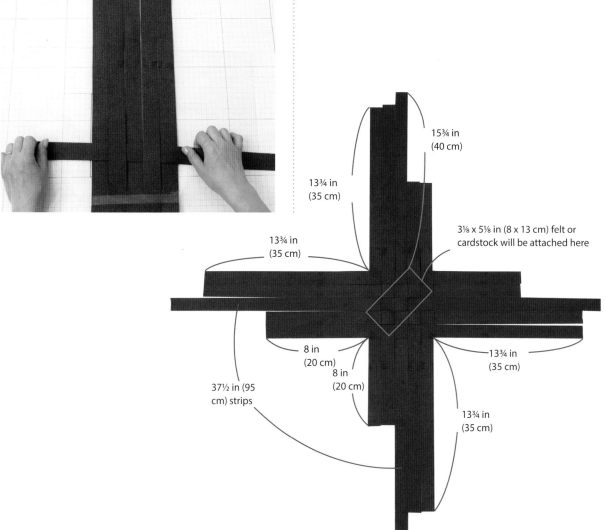

15¾ in (40 cm)

13¾ in (35 cm)

3⅛ x 5⅛ in (8 x 13 cm) felt or cardstock will be attached here

13¾ in (35 cm)

8 in (20 cm)

8 in (20 cm)

13¾ in (35 cm)

37½ in (95 cm) strips

13¾ in (35 cm)

## INSTRUCTIONS

**1.** Adhere the self-adhesive felt or glue the card stock to the wrong side of the woven work, so the 3⅛ in (8 cm) long edges face the shortest leather strips.

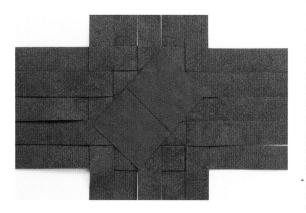

**2.** Cut a 5⅛ x 15¾ in (13 x 40 cm) and a 5⅛ x 23¾ in (13 x 60 cm) rectangle of satin self-adhesive fabric. Remove the release paper from the center portion of each piece by cutting a slit and peeling the paper back to expose the adhesive surface.

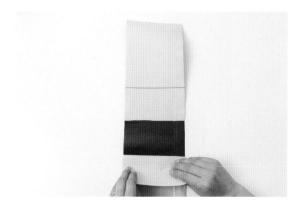

**3.** First, adhere the 5⅛ x 15¾ in (13 x 40 cm) rectangle to the wrong side of the woven work so it faces the short strips. Next, adhere the 5⅛ x 23¾ in (13 x 60 cm) rectangle so it faces the long strips.

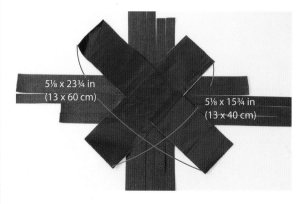

**4.** Fold the woven work around the self-adhesive felt or card stock attached in step 1 to form the bottom of the bag. Use clips or clothespins to temporarily hold the leather strips to the corners of the self-adhesive felt or card stock.

**5.** Next, weave the short side walls of the bag, working in an upward diagonal direction.

**6.** Completed view of one woven short side wall.

**7.** Fold the top two strip ends to the inside of the bag. Use clips or clothespins to temporarily hold the folds in place. These will be the "cat ears."

**8.** Use pieces of double-sided tape to secure the folded strip ends from step 7.

**9.** Remove the release paper and adhere the satin self-adhesive fabric to the short side walls of the bag. Trim any excess fabric.

**10.** Weave the long sides of the bag, working in an upward diagonal direction. Stop when they are equal in height to the short side walls.

**11.** Position the leather strips on a flat surface. Next, weave using the basic weaving technique until you reach the end of the strips (see page 22).

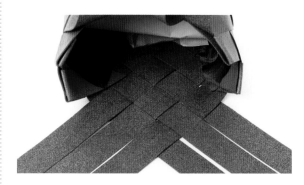

**12.** Use cellophane tape to temporarily secure the ends. Mark a cutting line 3⅛ in (8 cm) from the edge of the bag.

**13.** Cut a 5⅛ x 2 in (13 x 5 cm) rectangle of satin self-adhesive fabric. Adhere half of the satin self-adhesive fabric 1 in (2.5 cm) below the cutting line to secure the weave. Trim only the woven work along the cutting line, then fold the rest of the satin self-adhesive fabric around the edge and adhere.

**14.** Repeat steps 11–13 to weave the other long side of the bag and finish the edge with satin self-adhesive fabric.

**15.** On each side of the bag, thread the woven leather through the metal purse frame and fold to the inside so it is equal in height to the short side walls.

**16.** Remove the release paper from the satin self-adhesive fabric rectangle remaining from step 3.

**17.** Adhere the satin self-adhesive fabric to each long side wall of the bag. Trim any excess fabric.

**18.** Use the swivel hooks to clip the purse chain to the loops on the purse frame.

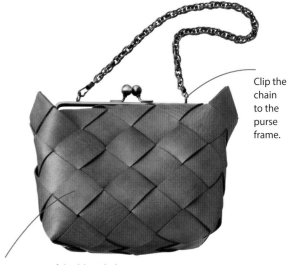

Clip the chain to the purse frame.

Use pieces of double-sided tape to secure any loose strips within the woven bag.

# LIBRARY TOTE

Shown on page 18

## MATERIALS

### For the Dark Variation

Color A: 15¾ yd (14.4 m) of 1¼ in (30 mm) wide faux leather strips in dark brown

Color B: 13¼ yd (12 m) of ⅝ in (15 mm) wide faux leather strips in chestnut brown

2¼ yd (2 m) of waxed cord in dark brown

### For the Light Variation

Color A: 15¾ yd (14.4 m) of 1¼ in (30 mm) wide faux leather strips in sand

Color B: 15¾ yd (14.4 m) of ¼ in (5 mm) wide suede cord in brown

2¼ yd (2 m) of waxed cord in beige

### For Both Variations

14¼ x 23¾ in (36 x 60 cm) of satin self-adhesive fabric

Eight rivet sets

## FINISHED SIZE: 12¾ x 11–11½ in (32 x 28–29 cm)

## GETTING STARTED

### For the Dark Variation

**1.** Cut ten 47¼ in (120 cm) long strips of each color of leather.

**2.** Arrange the strips at a 45° angle with the right side facing up, alternating Color A and Color B. Secure with cellophane tape.

### For the Light Variation

**1.** Cut 12 47¼ in (120 cm) long strips of each color of leather.

**2.** Arrange the strips at a 45° angle with the right side facing up, alternating two strips of Color A and Color B. Secure with cellophane tape.

# INSTRUCTIONS

**1.** Weave using the basic weaving technique, until the work measures about 27½ in (70 cm) long (see page 22).

**2.** Apply satin self-adhesive fabric to the wrong side of the woven work to create a lining, leaving ¾ in (2 cm) margins extending on all sides. Fold each edge of the woven work over 1¼ in (3 cm) and adhere to the lining margins to finish the edges.

**3.** Fold the woven work in half. Use waxed cord to hand stitch the sides of the bag, as shown on page 36.

**4.** Cut two 27½ in (70 cm) long strips of the 1¼ in (30 mm) wide faux leather. To make the handles, run the ends of each strip under the weave near the top corners of the bag. Secure the handles in place with rivets and tuck the ends inside the seams of the bag, as shown below.

Use two rivets to secure each handle end.

Use an awl or stiletto to insert the handle ends into the side seams of the bag. If necessary, use glue to secure.

# DESIGN YOUR OWN PROJECTS

All of the projects in this book are made with two simple techniques: basic weaving and braid weaving. With the basic weaving technique, both the right and wrong side of the leather will be visible in the finished project. This unique characteristic allows you to create a two-tone effect using only one color of leather strips. Or, you can use multiple colors of leather strips to create a variety of patterns, including stripes, diamonds, and houndstooth checks, all based on the way you arrange the strips prior to weaving. Refer to the guides on pages 96–99 for pattern and color inspiration when designing your own projects.

These coin purses are constructed with the basic weaving technique. You can easily alter the number and length of strips to customize the size and shape of your coin purse. Refer to the Classic Coin Purse instructions on page 54 for the basic construction method.

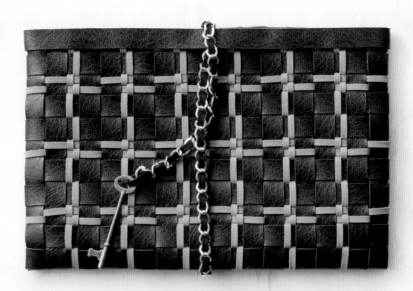

These clutches are made with the braid weaving technique and were inspired by the Bow Clutch design featured on page 60. Different thicknesses and colors of leather strips were used to create the fun houndstooth pattern.

Only the right side of the leather will be visible on projects made with the braid weaving technique. With this method, you can construct a three-dimensional bag as you weave, without the need for added sewing. This method is ideal for structured bags.

Once you master these two simple weaving methods, I hope you'll be inspired to design your own bags and accessories with interesting color combinations, patterns, and other design elements. Use the general construction steps of the projects included in the book as a jumping off point, then incorporate your own unique twists…the possibilities are endless!

# WEAVING DIFFERENT WIDTHS

You can use the basic weaving technique to produce complex-looking patterns just by using leather strips of varying widths.

## PATTERN A

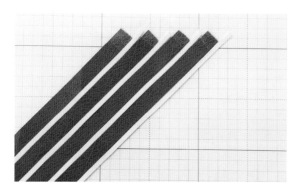

**1.** Alternately arrange a wide and a thin strip of leather. Use a total of four strips of each type of leather.

**2.** Weave the leftmost wide strip, then the leftmost thin strip using the basic weaving technique shown on page 22.

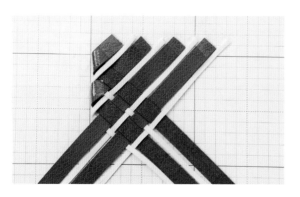

**3.** Continue weaving the wide and thin strips in sets.

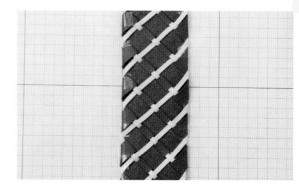

**4.** Follow the same process to complete the work using Pattern A.

# PATTERN B

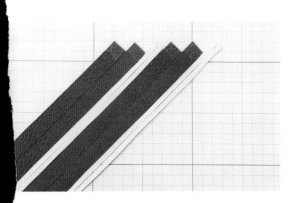

. Alternately arrange two wide and two thin trips of leather. Use a total of four strips of each type of leather.

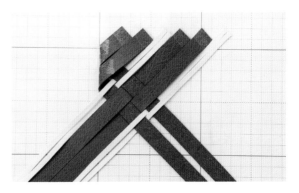

**2.** Weave the two leftmost wide strips using the basic weaving technique shown on page 22.

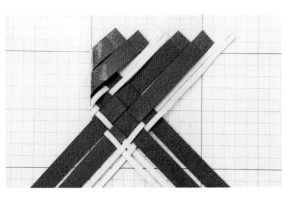

**3.** Next, weave the two leftmost thin strips.

**4.** Follow the same process to complete the work using Pattern B.

# WEAVING WITH DIFFERENT COLORS

One of the advantages of the basic weaving technique is the large variety of colorful patterns that can be created based on the starting arrangement of the leather strips. The following guide includes a few of my favorite patterns in the hopes that you'll be inspired to incorporate them into your own original projects. Experiment with your favorite colors to create new looks using these patterns.

## TWO COLOR PATTERNS

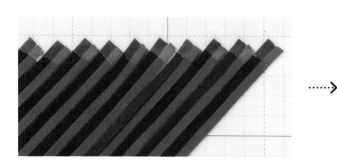 

Alternate blue strips and red strips.

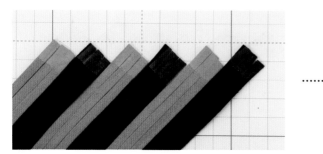 

Alternate three camel and three black strips.

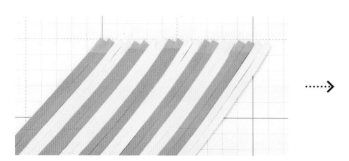 

Alternate two pink and two ivory strips.

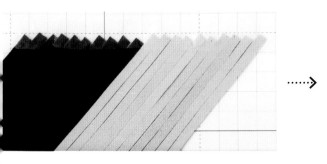

Alternate ten black and ten beige strips.

## THREE COLOR PATTERNS

Arrange strips in the following order: five taupe, four red, two blue, four red, and five taupe.

Arrange strips in the following order: two red, two brown, four caramel, and two brown. Repeat this pattern again for a total of 20 strips.

# ABOUT THE AUTHOR

Born in Tokyo, Naoko Minowa studied home economics in college and graduated with a degree in dyeing. In 2011, she opened Studio A Week, a hand weaving and vegetable dyeing shop, school, and gallery. Naoko is the chairwoman of the Japan Senshoku Association, which celebrates the traditional Japanese art form of fabric dyeing. She is also the author of *Finger Weaving Scarves & Wraps*.

# RESOURCES

Emmaline Bags
www.emmalinebags.com

Etsy
www.etsy.com
You can find leather strips, purse findings, and leather craft tools in independent shops on Etsy

Joann
www.joann.com

Hobby Lobby
www.hobbylobby.com

Lacis
www.lacis.com

Michaels
www.michaels.com

Rocky Mountain Leather Supply
www.rmleathersupply.com

Tandy Leather
www.tandyleather.com